DETOXIFYING LEADERSHIP

DETOXIFYING LEADERSHIP

My First Class Seat To Toxic Leadership

SUZANNE GRAHAM ANDERSON MBA, MSOL

Positively Suzanne

*Inspire * Motivate * Empower*

Positively Suzanne LLC

DETOXIFYING LEADERSHIP

My First Class Seat To Toxic Leadership

A book by

Suzanne Graham Anderson MBA, MSOL

Published by Positively Suzanne LLC.

Positively Suzanne

*Inspire * Motivate * Empower*

To contact the author through Positively Suzanne LLC, please email at suzanne@positivelysuzanne.com or visit their website at www.positivelysuzanne.com
ISBN: 978-1-7357369-0-7

Acknowledgement

First and foremost, I have to give credit to God, everything that I am, every blessing that I have is because of him!

I also have to honor my late dad Edward! He taught me the value of education and hard work. To my mother Doreen, who endured so much and sacrificed even more for me and my siblings. Your combination of love, values, discipline, and sacrifice made me into the person I am today.

To my husband, Paul, who is my biggest supporter, thank you for saying okay to every wild crazy dream I have, and for believing that I can accomplish anything! Well, except to give directions, but everything else you are my #1 fan! To my girls Sarah Jessica, and Sophia Grace, who believes that mommy can change the world! From the moment I laid eyes on each of you, I knew I wanted to give you the world, and I also knew that you would both change the world!

To my siblings, me being a middle child, had no choice but to practice being a leader early on! Donna, Jean Marie, Sidonie, Clifford, Edward, Alicia, and Andrew, each in your own way have inspired me by your strength, your resilience, adaptability, and talents.

I also have to acknowledge all the teachers that pushed and encouraged me; all the leaders that saw something in me, and all the friends that encouraged me. I thank you all for every encouragement, every prayer, and every listening ear.

Foreword

There is a debate that I have heard often, and it asks, *are great leaders born or are they created?* Wherever you fall in this debate, I hope that you can agree that a great leader can inspire their team to do great things, and a toxic leader can de-motivate a team and cause them to quit or be unproductive.

With over 20 plus *(yikes, did I say 20?)* years of experience as a leader, I was inspired to write this book for many reasons. I have had many leaders and many teachers! This book is a collection of some of the experiences that taught me, including the mistakes I made.

Another reason for me writing this book is that every company that I have been with has introduced a leadership book. Some of them are light reading and quite helpful while some are large tomes that you cannot connect with. But once in a while, you will find a book that inspires you, one that gives you some tips and insights on how to navigate being a leader and come out of it with your sanity intact. I am hoping this book does that for you! It is a collection of experiences that shaped me, but did not break me, that pushed me to be the best version of a leader I could be, and that is one that is consistently seeking growth.

And finally, this is for every little girl that was called bossy, stubborn, demanding, aggressive, assertive, and too much. Please know that you are just enough, and you are unstoppable. May you be the leader you aspire to work for.

Contents

The five stages of grief...4

A star is born...8

The I can do everything by myself leader......................9

This is the way it has always been done.........................11

The do as I say but not as I do leader............................13

The over sharer...15

The it's all about me leader..17

The inconsistent leader..18

The micro manager leader..20

The mirror leader...21

The absolute worst leader..22

The mentor...24

Leadership styles...26

Tips to practice to avoid being a toxic leader.................29

The Five Stages of Grief

He is an IMBECILE, a complete moron. I wonder how he got his job. He must have known someone on the staff or how else could he explain reading my paper and giving me a low grade. I know that there are five stages of grief but in that moment, there were only two, anger and burn him to the ground. Okay, it sounds a tad dramatic, but you have to understand where I was coming from.

Hi, my name is Suzanne and I like to get A's in all my classes! Now, that you know who I am, let me tell you about this professor who dared to give me a poor grade. I was at the tail end of wrapping up one of my degrees and I wrote a paper that I thought was pretty good. But, when I checked my grade, I found that the professor had given me a low grade. *(Okay quick side note,* this is something I learned. You should write every paper with the expectation of getting an A, but it is very important when you start a class that your first few papers are outstanding. This way, you have created a precedent for excellent papers, and writing anything less is unacceptable to you, because both you and your professors expect it, so something inside you rebels against putting out anything less than excellent). This is not a scientific method, but it has worked for me.

Okay, back to this professor who did not warrant an Amanda Bynes appeal to the president to change the grade, but at the very least deserved a strongly worded email to the Dean of Students.

Like I said, I was wrapping up my degree and I had maintained a perfect GPA, so I expected the trend to continue. When I checked my score, I saw red because I did not think it deserved a low grade, and I immediately went looking outside for an explanation. I checked out his Teacher's Bio and found out that he worked full-time, and he was only an Adjunct. So, that explained it, I thought. I then read all of his emails and announcement to the class looking for errors to validate that he would not recognize a well-written paper if he saw one.

After telling my husband, who was not appropriately horrified by this travesty, he had the nerve to suggest that I let it go and focus on the next paper. *(Quick side note again,* I knew if I filed for divorce then, I am sure that judge would have sided with me for having a partner who did not understand the great wrong that was done to me). After a few hours passed, I calmed down significantly, and I decided to read the professors feedback on why he gave me a low grade, (WHO KNEW).

In the course of one afternoon, I ran the full gamut of the five stages of grief.

Denial – I cannot believe he has the nerve to give me a low grade. Who does he think he is? Does he know who I am? Does he know that I only get A's?

Anger – He is an idiot. Clearly, anyone could see that it was an "A" paper. I will make sure he understands the consequences of giving a me a low grade. The Dean will hear from me and when this class is over, I hope he is ready for my feedback.

Bargaining – If I ask him to give me an opportunity to rewrite the paper, then I can change my grade. I will email him and ask him about the grade.

Depression – OMG, I cannot believe that I have such a low grade. Not only will it mess up my GPA, but it will be in my record and I will know that I did not graduate with a perfect GPA.

Acceptance – Okay calm down, it is one low grade: it is not the end of the world. It was your first paper in the class, and you have the entire semester to change your grade.

Once I read his feedback, I was pretty much in the acceptance phase. The instruction for the paper was to write about a company of my choice, talk about what I liked about the company, what I thought they did well, and where they had opportunities to improve. His feedback was that I was to remove myself from the paper. Huh, I was to remove everything out of the paper that was of my opinion and to use facts and data. (**Turns out I had overlooked that tiny piece of the instruction which turned out to be the most important part**).

This will serve you well as a leader, ensure that you pay attention to all the information given before you decide. Also, it is important that when you make a decision, it is not based purely on emotions.

The professor wanted me to remove everything in the paper that said I or me and focus on the company. The next week, I wrote a paper and I took everything out that referenced I or me. After doing that, I got an A and the teacher called it excellent! The AHA moment was that it was not until I removed everything out of the paper that was about me, that I got an excellent job.

And that is the same thing with leadership. When you remove everything about yourself in your daily tasks and decisions, and you focus on the people that you lead while making it about them, then and only then can you go from bad to excellent. That is how you stop yourself from becoming a toxic leader.

I have had a lot of leaders over the years, the good, the bad and the toxic. In their own way, each of them taught me something about leadership, even if it was what I should not do.

A Star is Born *(Well kind of)*

We all know the story of the stunning Naomi Campbell who was discovered at the age of 15 by a modelling agent while she was shopping. She went on to become one of the most iconic super models ever, setting trends and breaking barriers and is still working today. Well, my story is exactly like that, except for the stunning supermodel who was discovered while shopping and who went to on to fame and wealth. Okay, well maybe it is not like that at all, but in my mind that is how I saw it. I was working at a Dry Cleaners and a young manager that worked in retail saw me and thought I was fabulous and felt that I would do well in retail. He knew of a company that was hiring and he thought I would fit right in!

I went to the interview and when they asked if I had any retail experience, I responded no, but I was a fast learner. Two weeks later, I was promoted to assistant manager. I had a wonderful manager who was eventually promoted to another store, and I was promoted to Store Manager. Thus, a retail management career was born! Unfortunately, my first-class seat to some very toxic leadership behaviors also began!

The I Can Do Everything by Myself Leader

I had a leader that was a hard worker. There was nothing that she would not do in the store. She worked so hard that the team did not have to work as hard. She ran herself ragged, but she thought that was the way to show her people that she was not lazy.

There are many factors that go into play when you are promoted within a store, and you are suddenly supervising people that were your peers the day before. There is always that fear that people will think you are full of yourself. Therefore, you try to prove that you are not, by showing them that you are not going to suddenly turn into a dictator. My previous leader had also set the standard of doing everything on her own. Therefore, it was not a hard pattern to fall into.

I made sure I did everything, big projects, small projects and made up projects. I was determined to prove to everyone that I was a hard worker. When you set out to prove a point, often times you will prove it. I worked from open to close, I worked on my days off, and I worked overnight shifts even though the store was closed. I even worked during my vacations. I am happy to report that I did it, I proved to everyone that I was a hard worker. But I was worn out, burnt out, overworked, overtired, unmotivated, and sick of my job. Here is another thing working like that did, it showed everyone that I would work hard so they do not have to. Come to think of it, that should have been my motto: *"I will work hard so you don't have to."*

The lazy people were okay with me working hard. The ones that were not that invested just accepted that I worked hard. But the people who wanted to learn, who wanted me to teach them, got frustrated because they were more like props.

This was another big AHA moment, it was not about me. As a leader my job was to teach, and I was not teaching anyone. I was doing it all, and my doing all the work was not helping them. They were not learning and developing, they were not learning new skills daily. Instead, they were there to witness my **one man show**.

Here is the deal with the I can do it all by myself mentality as a leader. Your people will learn nothing, and if your people learn nothing, then you will continue to do more. You will continue to work on your days off and vacations because you have not equipped them to function without you, and that is doing them a disservice. Being a leader is more than you doing it all. When you are able to take your days off as a leader, or take a vacation and be confident that your team will be able to handle it in your absence, that is the goal and that is the win. As a leader, it is a credit to you the less your people need you, and the more independent they are. One should never be proud to say that their team is useless without them because then they have truly failed them. Teach them, not so you will do less, but that they will do more and that is how they will grow. Your people's ability reflects on you as a leader and if they cannot do anything without you, then you have taught them nothing.

The *This Is The Way* It Has Always Been Done

We have all heard the saying *if it ain't broke, don't fix it.* I am here to tell you to fix it even if it ain't broke. This expression to me is the same as the phrase, that is the way it has always been done. I think leaders get complacent if things are running smoothly and they end up believing that means no changes ever. Years ago, I took on the role of a District Manager for a popular retail brand and at the time I signed on because of their promise of changing the way things were done. I truly believe they could have changed and gotten better results, but everything I tried to do was thwarted by the mindset of this is the way we always did it, from all levels. And although I was recruited for my expertise, they balked each time I tried to use my expertise and reverted to the way it was always done. And yet, they were shocked that they were getting the same results. I tried to make changes and show them the way, but it seems the more I pushed, the more they dug in their heels, preferring to stick to the known versus the unknown.

Here is the deal with that phrase, you cannot grow if you do not do things differently. Even if the results are great, there's always room for improvement. This is why leaders like Steve Jobs and Michael Jordan were so admired. They were not satisfied with the best, but they sought excellence and despite stellar numbers, they kept seeing how far they could push not only themselves but those that worked with them.

If you ever find yourself uttering that phrase, I want you to stop. It is demotivating and will make some people not want to try. If people keep hearing a chorus of that phrase, they will stop sharing new ideas and you will not have growth.

Okay, I might be showing my age, but I remember AOL dial up and My Space. What if people were satisfied with that and had not tried anything else because it was the way it was always done. Today, we can be online in seconds, no dial up, no getting kicked off when someone calls on the line. Facebook, Instagram, and Twitter are instant and at our fingertips because of our smart devices. We have unprecedented access to news, influencers, celebrities, funny videos, and of course Oprah. Just think if they had uttered that phrase, we would not be able to keep up with the Kardashians and that would indeed be a tragedy.

The Do As I Say, But Not As I Do Leader

I will always remember the lecture from my doctor about not smoking, while he was smoking. Even as a child, I did not think it made sense but luckily, I was never tempted to smoke because I did not think it was cool. *(Okay I will save this lecture for another book).*

I had a boss who I liked, who everyone liked! He was a funny, likable guy, but he was unfair. He broke the rules often, and at first it seemed like he was a cool boss. He did not sweat the small stuff, but it turns out that the small stuff was important. He would come to work late every day and he would take long lunches. He would leave early, and he would stay in the office all day. At first, this did not bother me, but I realized I no longer had any urgency to being at work on time. Now this was dangerous because I had always struggled with being on time. But, seeing his lack of punctuality, I did not make any great effort to being on time. Until one day when I came to work late, he said I cannot come to work late. Rather, I had to lead by example and be on time. *(Wait what)?* I thought it was a fluke until I was late again, and he said it to me. I found out that he said it to another person about them being on time.

At first, I was angry that he had the gall to tell me to be on time when I cannot remember a time that he was on time. Then I realized that it was not about him and it was about how I wanted to be as a leader.

I realized that I expected my people to be on time, so I needed to lead by example and be on time, regardless if he was on time. He was comfortable being late and holding others accountable to being on time, but I was not okay with that. I realized that in looking to him, I was on the verge of being him. This is a very important lesson to learn because you have to follow the rules. You cannot hold your team accountable to the rules while you are comfortable bending them. That makes you hypocritical and your team will have no respect for you. The same rule applies to everyone, especially when you are the boss. It is important for your team to see you doing the right thing, and it is important to hold yourself to a higher standard. It should not be that I do this, but you cannot. Even motivated team members will get frustrated with this type of leadership.

The Over Sharer

In this technological era, we have gotten used to knowing more about others than we sometimes know about ourselves. Thanks to the paparazzi, tabloid media and social media, we have more information than we will ever need to know about many people. We are in an information overload era.

I have had a few leaders that overshared their personal lives. The entire team knew what was happening at home and in their relationships every day. The team celebrated with them on the good days, offered comfort on the bad days and walked on eggshells on the uncertain days; not knowing if they should offer a word of support on sisterhood or a call to arms to lock up all men. It can be very stressful. As much as you might think, your team is there for you. They are not your personal sounding board and should never be drawn into your relationship dramas. Your team needs to come to work and work, not try to offer advice on your relationship, not offer hugs, high fives or react to whatever is happening in your relationship that day.

It's okay to be human and you can share a milestone like weddings, births, deaths etc., but there is a limit to the things you share with your team and listening to your life story every day is not a great place for team members to be. Believe me, hearing about my boss's bikini wax was not something I thought I would have to sit through.

There were many pitfalls to this type of leadership because the team no longer respected the leader. The team felt they could offer advice to the leader about their life and it made it very uncomfortable when the significant other called or came by, and they had to pretend to know nothing. Also, this often times plays out with the team not respecting what the leader says about the business because they feel that if they cannot run their personal life then how can they run a business. I know you are thinking that is not always true, but I did not make the rules, I just happen to witness the toxic results, firsthand.

The It's All About Me, Leader

We have all heard the term, there is no I in team, but have you ever worked with someone who took the M and the E in team and turned it into ME. Unfortunately, I have had a few leaders like that. I have always been a hard worker and no matter the role I gave my best. However, it got very frustrating very fast when my leaders, who were supposed to teach me, spent more time in a competition with me that I was not even aware that I was in. Every success I achieved, they tried to diminish and when we had corporate visitors, they took all the credit. One particular leader was always in my corner and supported my growth until I became her peer and then it was a battle to death to win against me. Here is the sad part, I credited my success to her because she helped guide and push me. Unfortunately, she was so blinded by envy that she did not see that when I was complimented that she was complimented, too. Ultimately, I was a direct result of her influence!

No one wants to work for someone who takes all the credit and none of the blame; someone who makes it all about them and not about the team. A great leader understands that the success of the team is a direct reflection on them and if the team is successful, then they are successful.

The Inconsistent Leader

Now, this is the church girl in me coming out, but there is a scripture in the Bible (James 1:8) that says, *"A double minded man is unstable in all his ways."* (KJV) I think this is an apt description because the Inconsistent Leader is quite unstable to their team. The team is unsure of who they are dealing with on each day. The leader is never sure who to be because one day they are friendly, one day they are supportive, one day they are emotional and then one day they are volatile. Okay, you get the idea! I will stop with the adjectives. It was very difficult working for someone that mercurial, and instead of making it interesting, it felt like I was working in a field littered with land minds, and one misstep could cause an explosion. On one occasion, when working for such an individual, I gave my notice and they begged me to stay. They convinced me that they could not do it without me. Okay, so forgive me, but I fell for the flattery! However, when the inconsistency continued, I gave my notice again and this time I did not fall for the flattery. Within minutes of me resigning, she was on the phone with my assistant begging her to take my place and reasoning that now that I was gone, she could really soar since I was holding this assistant back. Interestingly enough, when she was speaking to me, she told me to cut the assistant loose because she was the only blot on my otherwise spotless career. Unfortunately, for her, my assistant respected me as a leader and gave her notice immediately.

I cannot stress enough how important consistency is in a leader. You will have to shift and adapt to the team you are leading, but your personality should not change. You cannot be their best friend one day, the disciplinarian the next, the dictator the next and so on. It is exhausting to keep up with all those personality changes and the team needs consistency in order to succeed. Your style can change depending on the situation, but your personality should not. Another valuable lesson I learned from this leader was the importance of integrity. Based on her action, I felt validated in my decision to leave, because she also did irreparable damage to our working relationship. I would not accept a position at a different company if I knew she was working there. Extra tip here, when someone leaves, do not burn the bridge to the ground because you never know when you might cross paths again. Handle every interaction with integrity.

The Micro Manager Leader

There are some people that are okay with being micro-managed, but I am not one of them. I had a leader who was a micro manager. She was constantly looking over my shoulder, checking everything I did, reading every email, checking every project, listening to every phone call, and having me submit every written document for approval. This got very frustrating because I felt stifled. It felt as if she had no faith in my abilities. Although time after time, I proved to her that I was quite capable of doing my job, I finally figured out that it had nothing to do with me. Rather, it was the only way she knew how to be. She had to control every aspect of the job and letting go was not something she could do. Luckily, I moved on from that role. It was very tough to grow under her leadership because I felt like she was constantly watching me and waiting for me to mess up. Whether that was her intentions or not, it became the result and the team would look forward to the days when she was off. This was bittersweet because they knew that she would be even more of a micro-manager after a day off.

I learned this term a long time ago in retail and that is, *trust but verify*. At some point, you are going to have to trust your team to do their job. As a leader, it is your job to verify that the work is done, but you should not control every aspect of the job. Work with them to develop their skill sets, but then empower then to make decisions and make mistakes that they can learn and grow from.

The Mirror Leader

This might sound like a strange one, but the Mirror Leader is the one that wants everyone on the team to look, think and act like them. It is like they are looking in a mirror and they want to see themselves reflected there. I had a leader like this, and it was tough because I am proud of my identity and my uniqueness. It was very different from hers. So, we often disagreed because she wanted me to do exactly what she would do. The danger with hiring people that mirror you is that you shut yourself off from learning and growing because you only want answers and solutions that reflect what you would do. There is no one person who has all the answers. Therefore, there is no point in asking for a solution if you are only going to use your solution.

Can you imagine how boring the world would be if everyone looked like you, spoke like you, acted like you, and thought like you? Come to think of it, history has given us some very devastating stories of people who tried to make a world like that. While the workplace did not come to that extreme, no one even bothered with an opinion because the only opinion she wanted was her own. Do you remember that fairytale, mirror mirror on the wall, who is the fairest of them all? Well, you know from the story that if she was not the fairest, it was death to all who were. Yep, sometimes a leader can be just like a fairy tale, except you never get Glenda the Good Witch. It is always the Evil Stepmother, the bitter crone, or the Wicked Witch of the West.

The Absolute Worst Leader

I know you were looking for a witty title, but unfortunately this leader represented all that is bad with toxic leadership. She was racist, she was sexist, and she hated leaders that knew more than her. She hated women who looked better than her, she hated men that were confident, and she hated kids. I had the displeasure of working with such a leader and it was very hard to please her. She found an issue with everything and was never pleased. She was critical if you were a parent, critical of your faith, critical of your dress and critical of your closeness with other leaders. She demanded absolute loyalty and she did nothing to inspire it. She wanted you to place your job above all else including family, health, faith and if you did not, she told you that you made the wrong choice. Okay, maybe she was a dictator.

She was so toxic that a conversation with her was torturous. As a leader, she spoke about one leader with another. She was a combination of all the bad leaders I have ever had rolled into one, and then some additional toxins. Many tried to report her, but she was friends with the head of HR so turning her in was very risky, and many left the company instead of tarnishing their reputation. After working with her for a very short time, I realized that such toxicity could not be instant, there had to be a trail. So, I did some investigation and found out that she had worked for several companies with roughly a year and a half each.

She had a pattern whereby she would start a role and several people would quit and then a few months later she would also leave. It was an open secret that she was a toxic leader, but she kept getting hired. I, ultimately, decided to leave the company because I could not work for her. Consequently, it highlighted something to me that companies need to do their due diligence when hiring leaders instead of just looking at their credentials. A toxic leader can set the tone for a company's culture, and not being aware is not a good reason for a toxic culture. As an organization, you are responsible for anyone in a supervisory role, so you have to ensure that the way they treat the team is consistent with the culture. It is important to check in, connect and most importantly to listen and follow up on all reports of toxic behavior.

The Mentor

Although I have had many toxic leaders, I wanted to end with a good example. I do not think this leader knows how much she impacted my life. In spite of me telling her that often, and over 20 years later, I still remember and implement what she taught me. The things that stood out for this leader was that she was fair, and she was always coaching in the moment, but not in a condescending way. She allowed you to find the answer and she led you to it by asking probing questions. She set goals and she held you accountable to them. She gave you feedback constantly, and she celebrated your accomplishments publicly as well as coached you in private. She inquired about your family and she remembered names and milestones. She shared details about her life but did not go in depth. She was a great coach who was tuned in to all the skill sets of her people, and she managed them accordingly in order to get the best out of all.

Today, we have many terms to describe great leadership. However, over 20 years ago, the thing that was the most impactful to our team was that our boss said what she meant, and she did what she said she was going to do. And to this day, that is a still a great trait to have as a leader!

In my over 20 plus year career as a manager and leader, I have had many bosses; more than enough to write several books. But, after many years of reading leadership books. I wanted to write one that did not go on too long, one that was not difficult to stay awake, and one that said the things you wished your friend told you.

There are managers and there are leaders, and both roles are important. There are times when you have to be a manager, and there are times when you have to be a leader. It is important that you know when to be either one.

Leadership Styles

Today, we have many different leadership styles, and here are some of the most common ones:

Autocratic – They are doing it their way.

Bureaucratic – They ensure the rules are followed and they do things by the book.

Charismatic – They rely on their charm and charisma to influence.

Democratic – They ask for and utilize input from others.

Laissez- faire – They are very hands off.

Servant – They are people first and believe that people are more productive when they feel personally and professionally fulfilled.

Situational – They utilize different styles based on the environment.

Strategic – They see the big picture and have a vision of what they want to accomplish, and they are able to motivate others to go after that vision.

Transactional – They reward based on performance.

Transformational – They inspire through effective communication.

It is important to know what type of leader that you are because the best leaders I have come across are the ones that knew who they were. They were able to use a combination of most, if not all of the styles to get results depending on what the situation was.

Growth is important as a leader, every day and every role gives you an opportunity to do that, never stop growing. Over the years, I have had many bosses, and many had the title of leader. However, I have learned that leadership is not a title, it is something that you are. I have learned from many people who did not have the title, but they were great leaders. I have learned from both the toxic leaders and the great leaders. I have learned from people I work with and I have learned from people who work for me. Basically, I am saying that you have to be open to learning no matter the source. As a leader, never stop learning, and learn from all sources.

My growth, as a leader, is still continuing because a leader should always seek growth. There is that great debate I mentioned in the beginning about whether a leader is born or made, and there are great points for either side, hence the debate. I can tell you this about me. I was born with certain innate qualities that others saw as leadership qualities. I was fair-minded, I stood up for others and I gathered facts before I decided. That, along with many other qualities, helped me. Over the years, I grew as a leader by being around other leaders, by being open minded, by being a better listener, by being flexible, by making mistakes and owning up to it, by being accountable and by not being afraid to fail.

Similar to the story I shared at the beginning, I consistently have to look within myself for answers to poor performance instead of looking for someone else to take the blame. I have to ensure that I have as much facts as possible before I decide. This is important because I had to remove the I mentality when leading a team. I had to learn that it is about me as a leader, but it is not about ME.

Tips to practice to avoid becoming a toxic leader

These are some tips that I have learned over the years from people that I admire and from mistakes that I made. But luckily, I learned from them:

- Communication has two parts; you have to talk, and you have to listen.
- It is more impactful to show your team who you are versus tell them.
- It is more about the people you lead and less about you.
- You are just as responsible for the worst performer on your team as you are for the top performer.
- Your team reflects you, both the good and the bad.
- You have to lead with accountability.
- Develop your team so they can be independent of you.
- Give praise and give it often.
- Feedback is an important part of development.
- Coach in private.
- You learn more when you listen.
- Do not be afraid to apologize.
- Failure is only one option.
- Work with people who challenge you.
- Work with people who inspire you.
- Before you fire someone, ask yourself if you gave them all the resources to succeed.
- Hire people that are different from you.
- Be transparent.
- Do not avoid the difficult conversations.
- Do not be afraid to ask for help.
- Never stop seeking growth.
- You do not have all the answers.
- You do not need to have all the answers.
- Do not be afraid to hire people that are smarter than you.
- IT IS REALLY NOT ABOUT YOU.